FROM SEA to SHINING SEA

MISSISSIPPI

BARBARA A. SOMERVILL

Consultants

MELISSA N. MATUSEVICH, PH.D.

Curriculum and Instruction Specialist
Blacksburg, Virginia

BRENDA PRITCHETT

Children's Librarian
Columbus-Lowndes Public Library
Columbus, Mississippi

MELISSA WRIGHT

Programming Consultant
Mississippi Library Commission
Jackson, Mississippi

CHILDREN'S PRESS®

A DIVISION OF SCHOLASTIC INC.

New York • Toronto • London • Auckland • Sydney • Mexico City
New Delhi • Hong Kong • Danbury, Connecticut

Mississippi is located in the Deep South. It is bordered by Tennessee, Alabama, Louisiana, Arkansas, and the Gulf of Mexico.

The photograph on the front cover shows Longwood Mansion in Natchez.

Project Editor: Meredith DeSousa
Art Director: Marie O'Neill
Photo Researcher: Marybeth Kavanagh
Design: Robin West, Ox and Company, Inc.
Page 6 map and recipe art: Susan Hunt Yule
All other maps: XNR Productions, Inc.

Library of Congress Cataloging-in-Publication Data

Somervill, Barbara A.
    Mississippi / by Barbara A. Somervill.
        p. cm. — (From sea to shining sea)
    Includes bibliographical references and index.
    ISBN 0-516-22392-5
    1. Mississippi—Juvenile literature. [1. Mississippi.] I. Title. II. Series.

F341.3 .S66 2003
976.2—dc21   2002015254

TABLE of CONTENTS

CHAPTER ONE

INTRODUCING THE MAGNOLIA STATE

Historic Stanton Hall in Natchez is one of many Mississippi homes built before the Civil War.

The word *Mississippi* comes from the Algonquian language and means "great river" or "father of waters." The state gets its name from the mighty Mississippi River, and rightly so. For centuries, the river, which forms the western border of the state, provided food, drinking water, and transportation for people who lived along its banks. Often, floods poured over the land and deposited rich soil for growing crops. The river gave Mississippi more than just a name; it gave the state life.

Mississippi is nicknamed the Magnolia State. The southern magnolia is both the state flower and the state tree. All year long, evergreen magnolia trees turn their leathery oval leaves to the sun. In springtime, snow white or pale pink blossoms perfume the air. Magnolias grow wild throughout the south, providing summer shade and winter greenery.

What else comes to mind when you think of Mississippi?

- The Biloxi lighthouse flashing warnings to ships in the Gulf of Mexico
- Shrimp boats pulling into Pascagoula, loaded with the day's catch
- Cotton growing under the hot Mississippi sun
- Musicians playing the blues
- Choctaw artists displaying their arts and crafts at the annual Choctaw Indian Fair
- Monuments honoring Confederate and Union soldiers at Vicksburg National Military Park
- Ballet dancers performing at the world-renowned USA International Ballet Competition in Jackson

Mississippi is the heart of the Deep South. It is catfish, Gulf Coast shrimp, and barbeque. It is ancient earth mounds and modern buildings. It is magnolia blossoms and jazz and blues. As you read this book, you will learn all about the great state of Mississippi—the Magnolia State.

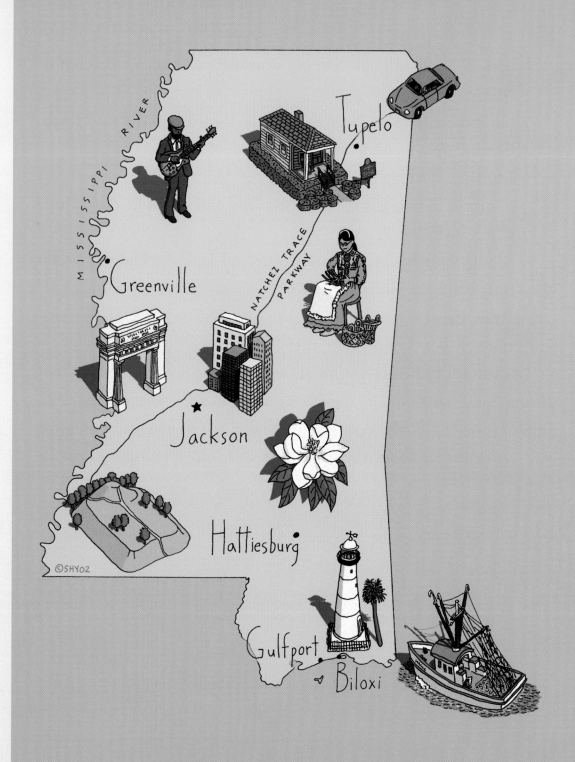

MISSISSIPPI RIVER

Tupelo

Greenville

NATCHEZ TRACE PARKWAY

Jackson

Hattiesburg

Gulfport

Biloxi

©SHY02

CHAPTER TWO

THE LAND OF MISSISSIPPI

Millions of years ago, Mississippi's land was part of the sea floor of a great ocean. Over time, the water receded and the land rose. As the ocean fell back, it left a large flat basin in the center of today's North America. Mississippi's land lies on the southern edge of this ancient basin.

Shaped like a shallow bowl, Mississippi's land is low and flat. The highest point—Woodall Mountain—is only 806 feet (246 meters) above sea level. The mean or average height of the state is just 300 feet (91 m), which is higher than only five other states.

Mississippi is nearly twice as long as it is wide. From north to south, the state stretches 352 miles (566 kilometers). At its widest point, east to west, Mississippi measures 188 miles (303 km). Alabama lies to the east of Mississippi. The state shares its northern border with Tennessee. The Mississippi River wiggles along the western border, separating

Dunn's Falls near Meridian is a 65-foot (20-m) waterfall that once powered a nearby mill.

Mississippi from Arkansas and Louisiana. To the south, the state has a small coastal area on the Gulf of Mexico.

A farmer stands in his cotton field in Mississippi. Cotton is used in many products, including clothing, sheets, and even dollar bills.

LAND REGIONS

There are three land regions in Mississippi. They are the Mississippi Alluvial Plain, the East Gulf Coastal Plain, and the Black Belt. The characteristics of each region vary greatly.

Mississippi Alluvial Plain

The Mississippi River affects all the land in the Mississippi Alluvial Plain, a narrow band along the western border of the state. This area is also called the Delta. At the mouth of the Mississippi River, the water divides and spreads out over a wide, triangular-shaped area, like the Greek letter Δ *(delta)*.

This is cotton country. The soil is rich, warm, and moist. It is ideal for growing the state's largest cash crop. The river often floods the land and deposits new soil rich in minerals. These floods make the soil fertile.

You'll find many oxbow lakes in the Alluvial Plain. Because the Mississippi is an old river, it meanders, or winds around. An old river flows more slowly than a young river. Over time, soil deposits, rocks, and logs build up dams in the river. They block the normal river flow and push the river in a different direction. As the river changes its course, it sometimes cuts off a short stretch of water and forms a lake. These lakes are U-shaped or the shape of an oxbow, the yoke or harness around an ox's neck. Among the region's oxbow lakes are Beulah, Moon, Lee, and Washington Lakes.

The Alluvial Plain also has bayous. These are low-lying, swamplike regions that are riddled with streams and small islands. Bayous are alive with fish, snakes, muskrats, and alligators. Insects thrive in the hot, damp climate of bayous. Crickets chirp and mosquitoes buzz through the night.

Marshy creeks called bayous are found in the Alluvial Plain.

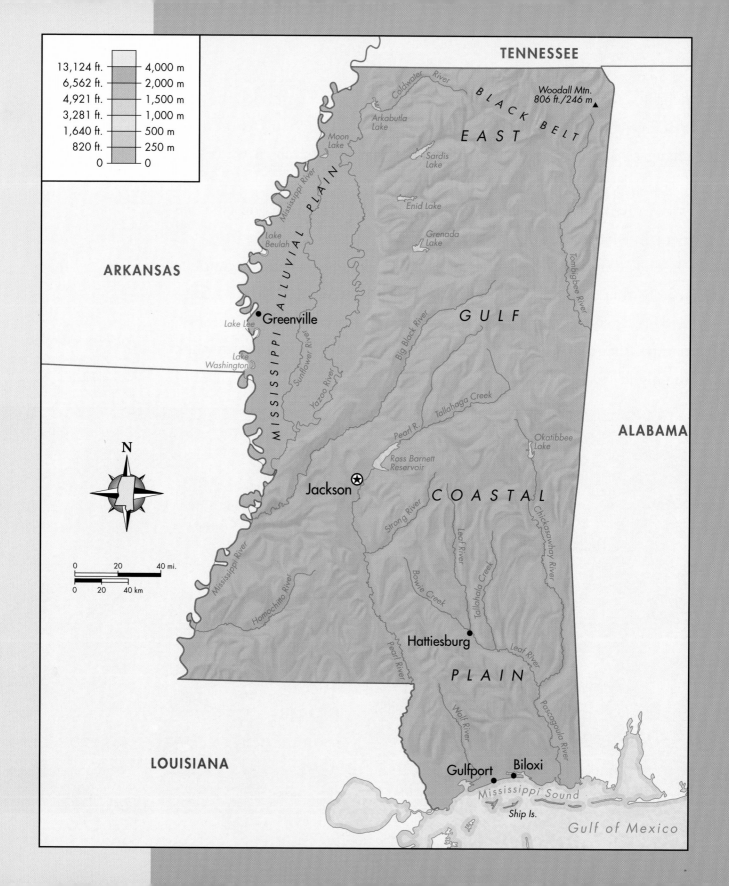

TENNESSEE

13,124 ft. — 4,000 m
6,562 ft. — 2,000 m
4,921 ft. — 1,500 m
3,281 ft. — 1,000 m
1,640 ft. — 500 m
820 ft. — 250 m
0 — 0

Coldwater River

Woodall Mtn.
806 ft./246 m ▲

B L A C K   B E L T

E A S T

Arkabutla
Lake

Moon
Lake

Sardis
Lake

ARKANSAS

M I S S I S S I P P I   A L L U V I A L   P L A I N

Enid Lake

Grenada
Lake

Tombigbee River

G U L F

Lake
Beulah

Mississippi River

Big Black River

Lake Lee
● Greenville

Sunflower River

Lake
Washington

Yazoo River

Tallahaga Creek

Pearl R.

Okatibbee
Lake

ALABAMA

N

Ross Barnett
Reservoir

C O A S T A L

Jackson ✪

Strong River

Leaf River

Chickasawhay River

0   20   40 mi.
0   20   40 km

Mississippi River

Tallahala Creek

Homochitto River

Bowie Creek

Leaf River

Pascagoula River

Hattiesburg ●

P L A I N

Pearl River

Wolf River

LOUISIANA

Gulfport ● ● Biloxi

Mississippi Sound

Ship Is.

Gulf of Mexico

10

East Gulf Coastal Plain

The East Gulf Coastal Plain covers about 9 in 10 acres (3.6 in 4 hectares) of the state. The region extends from the Gulf of Mexico to the Tennessee border. The land is covered with gently rolling hills, called the Cane or Bluff Hills. In the southeastern corner of the state lie the Piney Woods, which are hills covered with loblolly, slash, and longleaf pine trees.

The soil and climate in the Coastal Plain are ideal for growing fruits, vegetables, pecans, and sweet potatoes. There are also gypsum and salt mines in the southern area, as well as oil and natural gas. Gypsum is a mineral used to make paint, plaster, insulation, filters, and even candy.

The Black Belt

A long finger of dark, rich soil juts into the northeast section of the state. This is the Black Belt, which extends from Alabama into Mississippi. The Black Belt gets its odd name from the dark, nearly black soil. This is another region where cotton is still king of crops.

RIVERS AND LAKES

The major river in Mississippi is the one that gave the state its name. The Mississippi River originates in Lake Itasca, Minnesota. The river flows for 2,340 miles (3,766 km) down the center of the United States. It forms one of the largest river systems in the world when combined

A river tugboat pushes barges down the Mississippi River.

with the Missouri. The Mississippi-Missouri river system drains most of the Great Plains.

Mississippians worry about flooding almost every year. Heavy rains and melting snow in the north (Illinois, Minnesota, Iowa, Missouri, and other northern Midwest states) pour into the Mississippi River. As the river fills, it reaches flood stage—the point at which a river pours over its banks. To control floods, dams and levees (man-made riverbanks) have been built along the Mississippi's banks. When flooding threatens, Mississippians try to raise the riverbanks by adding sandbags to the levees. At times, the Mississippi is too strong to hold back. Its waters pour over the countryside, destroying homes, businesses, and crops.

The state of Mississippi is crisscrossed with many other rivers, streams, and small lakes. Other major rivers include the Yazoo, Big Black, and Tallahatchie, which all feed into the Mississippi. In the eastern part of the state, the Pearl River flows southward into the Gulf of Mexico, as does the Chickasawhay and the Pascagoula.

Most of Mississippi's lakes are man-made. They were created by damming rivers to form reservoirs, basins formed to hold water. The largest of these lakes is Ross Barnett Reservoir on the Pearl River. Smaller oxbow lakes are found along the western border of Mississippi.

The Pearl River serves as a boundary between the Gulf Coast portion of Mississippi and Louisiana.

PLANTS AND ANIMALS

Woodland covers slightly more than half of Mississippi. Much of this woodland is found in the state's six national parks and twenty-nine state parks. The state's many pines bear unusual names, such as loblolly and slash pine. Growing amid the pines are hardwoods, such as oak, hickory, tupelo, pecan, and sweet gum. Both soft and hardwoods are important to the state's lumbering industry.

EXTRA! EXTRA!

The Pascagoula is called the "singing river" because of the strange noise it makes as it flows. Legend says that when warriors of the Natchez tribe attacked the Pascagoula people, the Pascagoula held hands and chanted, and—even now—the river sings their song.

Spanish moss grows in many parts of the southeastern United States.

Gray beards of Spanish moss drape the branches of many Mississippi shade trees. Spanish moss has no roots and lives by taking moisture from the air. This odd, spongy plant was once used to stuff seat cushions and mattresses.

In springtime, magnolias and dogwoods sprinkle the woodlands with lacy, white blossoms. Bright pink azaleas, delicate camellias, and vivid redbuds grow wild throughout the forests. Vivid pink and purple crape myrtles bloom beneath the hot Mississippi summer sun.

Hummingbirds flit from blossom to blossom, drinking sweet nectar. The woodland is home to the mockingbird, the Mississippi state bird. You'll also find plenty of cardinals, turkey vultures, and small songbirds. Wild doves, turkeys, and quail provide excellent hunting throughout the state. Even the awkward pelican, with its huge beak and round belly, finds a home in Mississippi.

Mississippi's bayous shelter strange, slithering creatures that enjoy the damp, eerie swamp. Tall bald cypress trees grow straight out of the water and provide nest sites for many songbirds. Bald cypress trees are related to giant redwoods. They are evergreens with soft ruffles of needles on their branches.

Turtles, buffalo fish, bass, and catfish share the still bayou waters with alligators and a variety of poisonous snakes, such as the cottonmouth, water moccasin, and coral snake. There are also rattlesnakes and eastern indigo snakes. The indigo is on the endangered species list and is protected by law. Opossums and muskrats live on small islands throughout the swamp, called hummocks. These islands also provide homes for squirrels, rabbits, foxes, armadillos, and a few deer.

In 2001, a tornado hit the Pontotoc area, destroying hundreds of homes and businesses.

CLIMATE

Summers in Mississippi are hot and sweltering. There is relatively high humidity, which is the amount of moisture in the air. The average July temperature is 80° Fahrenheit (27° Celsius), although there are plenty of days when the thermometer lingers around 100° F (41° C). Dark thunderclouds roll in on many summer days, followed by heavy storms and dramatic lightning.

Mississippi has also endured some terrible storms. From spring through late summer, Mississippians watch for tornadoes. Tornadoes are whirling columns of air that form over land, usually from spinning thunderclouds. Tornadoes tear across the land at 25 to 40 miles per hour (40 to 64 kilometers per hour) with an air speed of up to 300 miles per hour (483 kph). Hurricane season lasts from midsummer through October. A hurricane is a storm that begins over water. Hurricanes spin at speeds ranging between 75 and 200 miles per hour (120 to 320 kph) and move at 10 to 20 miles per hour (16 to 32 kph).

Mississippi winters are mild, with few days on which the temperature drops below freezing. The average temperature in January is 45° F (7° C). However, there are rare days when frigid winter winds blow down from the north and chill the state. The lowest recorded temperature is −19° F (−28° C) at Corinth on January 30, 1966. There have been snow, hailstorms, and freezing rain in Mississippi, but these are not common.

Mississippi is wet. The average precipitation across the state is 56 inches (142 centimeters), which mostly falls as rain. The Gulf of Mexico is responsible for higher rainfall along the coast, which often amounts to about 70 inches (178 cm) per year. Water from the Gulf evaporates and forms clouds. When the clouds move over land, they deposit their water in the form of rain.

CHAPTER THREE

MISSISSIPPI THROUGH HISTORY

Almost twelve thousand years ago, the first people known to live in present-day Mississippi arrived. They were native people of the Hopewell culture, who settled along the Mississippi River. They came from regions to the north, also along the Mississippi River. The Hopewell people were excellent farmers who grew beans, squash, and corn. They are also known as Mound Builders because they built massive earth hills, or mounds, that served as cemeteries and religious temples.

Today, Emerald Mound, along the Natchez Trace Parkway, remains as a monument to the Mound Builders. The flat top of Emerald Mound is 35 feet (10.7 m) high and covers 8 acres (3.2 ha) of land. The mound was built about seven hundred years ago. People lived in a town around the mound until about A.D. 1600. These people were the ancestors of the Natchez tribe.

Emerald Mound may once have been used for religious rituals.

We do not know why the Hopewell culture disappeared, only that it was replaced by the Mississippian culture. From about A.D. 800 to 1500, the Mississippians formed one of the most advanced cultural groups of North America. They built roads, traded with other cultures, had an organized religion, and set up large cities. We know much about this culture because it was the custom to bury personal belongings along with a person's body. Scientists have uncovered and studied these items, including bracelets made from copper, beads, rings, earrings, statues of eagles and falcons, and tools. A man's possessions might include fishhooks, axes, or farm tools. A woman's grave may yield pots, nutcracking stones, and cooking utensils.

By the time Europeans arrived in the region, the Mississippian culture was declining. In its place were many Native American tribes. The three largest and most powerful tribes were the Choctaw, Chickasaw, and Natchez.

The Choctaw had the largest population. They lived in central and southern Mississippi. The Choctaw were farmers. They lived in huts built from mud and tree bark and formed small villages. They were closely related to the Chickasaw, who lived in the northern part of present-day Mississippi. The Chickasaw were hunters. To expand their hunting grounds, they sometimes fought against smaller, less powerful tribes, and even battled against the Choctaw, their close relatives. Both tribes spoke a variety of the Muskogean native language.

The Natchez lived in bayou country in the southwest area of Mississippi. They were farmers and fishers who lived in small villages. The

Natchez were closely related to the Mississippian culture. Both groups were sun worshippers and built earth mounds for religious rites.

The Choctaw and the Chickasaw were among the "Five Civilized Tribes," as they became known to European settlers. Europeans thought them "civilized" because these tribes adopted European ways, including building towns, farming the land, and creating town government.

Many early Native Americans in Mississippi built villages along the Mississippi River.

THE EUROPEANS ARRIVE

In 1540, Hernando de Soto of Spain became the first European to explore present-day Mississippi. De Soto traveled with a troop of armed soldiers. Although the Spanish met several native cultures, they were looking for gold and had no interest in the local people. The Spaniards treated the natives brutally. They killed many natives and beat others. They considered these killings to be a kind of sport. The native people hated the Spanish leader so much, that when de Soto died, his men sank his body in the Mississippi River rather than bury it. They were afraid the native people would dig up and destroy de Soto's body.

WHO'S WHO IN MISSISSIPPI?

Hernando de Soto (c.1500–1542) was a Spanish *conquistador*, or conqueror. He is credited with being the first European to explore much of the southeastern United States, including Georgia, Alabama, Mississippi, Tennessee, Oklahoma, and Louisiana. De Soto died of a fever and was buried in the Mississippi River.

La Salle claimed for France all the land in the Mississippi River Valley.

In 1682, Frenchman René-Robert Cavelier, Sieur de La Salle, traveled the length of the Mississippi River from present-day Illinois to the Gulf of Mexico. La Salle explored and claimed the land on both sides of the Mississippi River for his home country of France. This vast region was called *Louisiana,* after French King Louis XIV. Today's Mississippi was part of the Louisiana region. The French wanted the land for settlement and fur trading.

In 1699, another French explorer, Pierre le Moyne, Sieur d'Iberville, established the first permanent European settlement in Mississippi on Biloxi Bay along the Gulf Coast, called Fort Maurepas. (It was later renamed Old Biloxi, and is now called Ocean Springs.) Fort Rosalie, built by the French in 1716, would later become the town of Natchez. Toward the center of the state, LeFleur's Bluff was founded as a trading post for fur trappers along the Pearl River. This post grew into the city we now call Jackson.

Over time, people traveled from Europe to Mississippi hoping to find a comfortable life. However, they were sometimes disappointed. Life was difficult for these early pioneers. The settlers endured diseases such as malaria and typhoid fever, raging spring floods, and sweltering summers. They also faced hostile Native Americans, who fought against the settlers because of past history with Europeans. Native cultures passed down stories about the cruel Spaniards who overran their land, and tribes tried to prevent settlers from moving to Mississippi. The natives were often forced off their land by Europeans. Most native people believed that no one owned the land, and they could not understand why Europeans claimed land as their own. Despite these difficulties, however, colonists continued to settle in Mississippi.

WHAT'S IN A NAME?

What are the origins of some Mississippi names?

Name	Comes From or Means
Mississippi	Algonquian word meaning "great river" or "father of waters"
Picayune	Named by resident Eliza Nicholson; Nicholson's husband ran a newspaper that sold for half a dime—a picayune
Biloxi	Sioux word meaning "first people"
Jackson	Named for General Andrew Jackson
Oxford	Named after the English town of Oxford (home of the University of Oxford) in hopes that the state would build a university there
Tombigbee	Choctaw word meaning "coffin makers"

Europeans built log cabins to live in. They needed help from native tribes to survive living in the colony.

In the 1700s, Great Britain controlled the East Coast of North America from modern-day Georgia through Maine. Their holdings stretched westward to the Appalachian and Allegheny Mountains. During the same time, the French controlled most of the land west of the Appalachians, up to and including much of the Rocky Mountains and today's northwest United States. In 1722, the French set up a regional capital in the city of New Orleans.

The British realized the value of France's Louisiana territory and wanted to take over the land from the French. To do this, they needed the help of native people living in the region because the British did not have forts or outposts there. In the south, the British befriended the Chickasaw and Natchez tribes, providing the tribes with weapons. They wanted the tribes to attack French settlers and force them out of Mississippi. In 1729, Natchez warriors attacked Fort Rosalie and killed more than two hundred French settlers. Small battles with the native tribes followed and soon discouraged France, which pulled out of much of Mississippi.

By 1754, Great Britain's desire to expand westward led to war with France. The French and Indian War (1754–1763) was fought from the Ohio River Valley in

EXTRA! EXTRA!

One of the first major business events in Mississippi was a sneaky and cruel trick. In 1717, France's King Louis (above) granted John Law's Company of the West the right to develop part of Mississippi. Law described the new land as a paradise with fertile land, beautiful scenery, and great riches. His promise of such a marvelous homeland attracted French colonists who invested large sums of money to develop the colony. Law's lies became known as soon as pioneers landed and saw that their new paradise was actually wild, untamed land. In fact, much of Law's land was covered by swamp and was home to snakes and alligators. As a result, many French people lost the money they had invested. This incident affected the economy throughout France and became known as the Mississippi Bubble.

the north to the Mississippi Delta in the south. The war ended with the Treaty of Paris, which gave the British all land from the Mississippi River eastward, including present-day Mississippi.

A FIGHT FOR FREEDOM

The end of the French and Indian War gave Great Britain much land, but it also left the British owing large amounts of money for goods and soldiers' pay. In an effort to raise money, the British taxed the people living in the North American colonies. These taxes added cost to everything colonists bought, including playing cards, paper, glass, furniture, ink, sugar, and tea. The colonists rebelled, and the American Revolution (1775–1783) was fought to free the colonies from Great Britain's rule.

The war ended in British defeat and the formation of the United States of America. Northern Mississippi became a territory of the United States. Southern Mississippi, which was called West Florida at that time, was returned to Spain. The United States gained control of the western part of Florida in 1795. In 1798, the territory of Mississippi was officially formed with Natchez as its capital city.

Britain's victory in the French and Indian War opened the American West to development by British colonists.

FIND OUT MORE

Look at a map of the Louisiana territory and the British colonies in North America before the French and Indian War. Trace a line with your finger down the Mississippi River to see how much new land Britain gained in the Treaty of Paris. Was Britain's new territory about three times, five times, or ten times as large as the original colonies?

This painting by Dennis Malone Carter depicts the Battle of New Orleans. In this battle, Mississippians helped save New Orleans from the British during the War of 1812.

WAR, PEACE, AND STATEHOOD

In 1812, the United States was once again at war with Great Britain. This war started when British naval ships took sailors from United States ships and forced the sailors to serve in the British navy. This practice was called impressment.

During the War of 1812 (1812–1815), many Native American tribes chose to fight. They had developed friendships with settlers who lived in the area and fought by their side. The Choctaws fought alongside the Mississippians, while to the south the Creeks fought for the British. A force under the leadership of General Andrew Jackson eventually defeated the Creeks.

After the war, a large number of new settlers came to the Mississippi territory, which included the regions we know today as Mississippi and Alabama. By this time, the population of Mississippi had reached more than 60,000—the number required for a territory to become a state. On December 10, 1817, Mississippi became the twentieth state of the United States of America, leaving Alabama as a separate territory. David Holmes became the state's first governor. Natchez, Washington, and Columbia all briefly served as capitals from 1817 to 1822, when Jackson became the permanent capital.

KING COTTON

By 1830, the population of Mississippi was 136,621, nearly double what it had been ten years earlier. The state's rich soil and warm, moist weather was ideal for growing cotton, which was used to make clothing, towels, and bandages. Landowners grew cotton on plantations, or huge farms that grew one main crop. In Mississippi, that crop was usually cotton.

Plantations required large amounts of land, much of which was occupied by Native American tribes. In 1830, the United States government passed the Indian Removal Act, which forced native tribes to give up their land and resettle in Oklahoma, the newly formed Indian Territory. The Natchez, Pascagoula, and Chickasaw were among the native people forced to move. The Native Americans of Mississippi walked from their homeland to Oklahoma, a distance of about 600 miles (960 km). Thousands of native people died along the way from cold, hunger, and diseases. The Choctaw were the last to leave, but they, too, were eventually forced out to make way for white settlers. Only a small group of Choctaw refused to leave Mississippi.

FIND OUT MORE

The Five Civilized Tribes included the Choctaw and the Chickasaw. What were the other three tribes? What happened to these tribes?

Plantations were busy places that required many slaves to plant and pick cotton.

Together, the southern states formed a new nation called the Confederate States of America, separate from the United States. Jefferson Davis, a former United States senator from Mississippi, became the president of the Confederacy. In April 1861, Confederate forces fired on Union troops at Fort Sumter. The Civil War (1861–1865) had begun.

Mississippi provided both men and money for the Civil War effort. More than 80,000 Mississippians served in the Confederate army. In the beginning, the South appeared to be winning a quick victory. Mississippians thought the war would soon be over, based on news they heard about victories at the battles of First and Second Bull Run in Virginia. Even the battle of Shiloh, Tennessee, was reported as a victory, although that report was false. In her diary, Mississippi schoolteacher

Caroline Seabury recalled the anxiety of waiting for news: "April 6, 1862: Again we hear of the two great armies in battle at Shiloh— but little more than 100 miles from here. Still fighting on Sunday—"the day of battles"—"Our side completely victorious" is the last dispatch. Gens. Beauregard & Grant commanding. The suspense is heart-rending. Who can lie down and sleep quietly while such awful scenes are being enacted so near us?"

A group of Mississippians in the Confederate army practice for battle at their campsite.

Because of its key location on the Mississippi River and its position as a leader of the Confederacy, the Union army made Mississippi one of its key targets. The most important battle in the state took place at Vicksburg. Beginning in May 1863, Union General Ulysses S. Grant's forces laid siege to the city. The army stopped all supplies and people from going into or leaving Vicksburg. The people had to live on the food they already had in the city. The Confederate army could not get weapons, bullets, or medical supplies for injured soldiers. Forty-seven days later, on July 4, 1863, Vicksburg fell. Casualties on both sides numbered almost 20,000.

During the Vicksburg campaign, Grant's army fought several small battles in quick succession, winning at Port Gibson, Raymond, Jackson,

Confederate soldiers tried to defend Vicksburg, the last major river port still in Southern control in 1862.

Champion's Hill, and the Big Black River. Union General W. T. Sherman's troops supported Grant's successes elsewhere in the state. Sherman's army marched from Vicksburg to Meridian, the site of a major railroad distribution center for the South. This was important because it prevented the Confederate army from shipping men, weapons, and supplies to many southern cities. Mississippi fell to the Union onslaught. The losses in Mississippi tolled the beginning of an end to the Confederacy.

During the Civil War, about 25,000 Mississippians died, while an equal number suffered serious injuries. In April 1865, the Civil War ended, and it was time to rebuild. Just after General Robert E. Lee's surrender at Appomattox, President Lincoln was assassinated. Andrew Johnson was left with the awesome task of rebuilding both the Union and the shattered South.

RECONSTRUCTION

In March 1867, Mississippi fell under control of the United States military. Slavery had been abolished in 1863 by the Emancipation Proclamation. However, Mississippi needed to write a new state constitution, or set of rules to run the government, that included freedom for African-

Americans. After the constitution was adopted in 1870, Mississippi was readmitted to the Union. In that same year, Hiram Revels, an African-American minister, was chosen to represent Mississippi in the United States Senate. Revels filled the seat formerly held by Jefferson Davis. He was the first African-American to serve in the United States Senate.

As a senator, Hiram Revels fought for equal rights for all American citizens.

JIM CROW LAWS AND SHARECROPPING

Although African-Americans had made some progress, they didn't get far. Many southern whites had grown up with African-Americans as slaves, and they could not accept the idea of treating African-Americans as equals. It wasn't long before laws were created to make the class separation clear. The Mississippi state legislature passed laws that forbade African-Americans from using the same public facilities—restaurants, stores, schools, and rest rooms—as whites. The state government also made it extremely difficult for African-Americans to vote and own property. These laws were called Jim Crow laws, after a character in song-and-dance shows.

Southern plantation life had come to an end, but resourceful landowners came up with a new idea that kept former slaves chained to the land: sharecropping. Through sharecropping, a landowner and tenant signed a contract that allowed the sharecropper (tenant) to farm the land and pay the owner rent in the form of crops. Often, the sharecropper was a former slave of the landowner. The landowner provided land,

A sharecropper "settles up" his debt at a Mississippi general store.

The boll weevil affected cotton production throughout the 1900s.

seeds, tools, and food. The sharecropper did all the work. After the harvest, the landowner claimed his share, which was usually almost the entire crop. The rest was given to the tenant farmer. In this way, landowners grew rich off the labor of African-Americans—a situation not much different from slavery.

THE TWENTIETH CENTURY

In 1907, disaster struck Mississippi in the form of a small insect called the boll weevil. The boll weevil laid its eggs inside cotton bolls. Young weevils ate the cotton from the inside as they grew, and the cotton crop was slowly destroyed. Declining prices for cotton crops and reduced crop size made Mississippi, once a financial power, one of the poorest states in the country. The boll weevil problem still affects cotton farming in Mississippi, and the state is actively trying to get rid of this costly pest.

One way to help the state's finances was to develop new industries. The boll weevil disaster did have one benefit: Farmers were forced to find other crops to grow besides cotton. Agriculture branched out to include raising hogs, cattle, and poultry and growing soybeans, hay, and vegetables. New railroad lines were built that provided access to Mississippi's rich pine forests. Lumbering became an important industry in the state, along with textiles, the business of turning raw materials into cloth.

FIND OUT MORE

The textile industry is important to Mississippi's economy. What exactly are textiles? What textiles do we use in everyday life?

A CHANGING WORLD

In 1914, events took place in Europe that affected the entire world. The Archduke Ferdinand, a member of the Austrian royal family, was killed in Sarajevo, Yugoslavia. The killer was a Serbian. Austria-Hungary declared war on Serbia, and Germany joined the war as the friend or ally of Austria-Hungary. Serbia also had allies—England, France, and Russia. Within a short time, all of Europe was involved in what would become World War I (1914–1918).

When World War I began, the United States chose not to fight. However, manufactured products, such as cloth, guns, bullets, and canned food, were sold to England and France, and helped put Mississippians to work. In 1917, after United States ships were attacked by German submarines, the United States joined the war. About 65,000 Mississippians served in the armed forces. Many members of the military trained at Camp Shelby near Hattiesburg before shipping out to Europe.

World War I brought better times to Mississippi, but the improvement was short-lived. In 1927, the Mississippi River flooded. It was the worst known flood to ever hit the state. It began in Cairo, Illinois, and by the time it struck Mississippi, the raging water washed over river

The townspeople of Greenville walk on a temporary wooden sidewalk above the floodwaters.

cities and towns, destroying everything in its path. Particularly hard-hit were Greenville, Vicksburg, and Natchez. More than 100,000 people lost homes and property. To prevent further flooding, levees were built along the Mississippi River. However, the flood had cost the state millions of dollars, a large loss for a struggling economy to overcome.

Two years later, in 1929, the New York Stock Exchange crashed, sending the entire country into the Great Depression. Banks and businesses lost great amounts of money. People who had money in banks or invested in businesses also lost money. Poor states, such as Mississippi, were hardest hit, as cotton prices fell.

The state's workers struggled. Few people could afford to buy new houses, cars, machinery, or even clothing and food. Money problems hit industries hard. With no one to buy company products, factories closed, putting many people out of work. Lumber and textile mills had no place to sell their raw materials, so they, too, closed.

With no jobs, people could not pay for their homes or farms. Mississippi, like other states, struggled to free itself from the grip of poverty brought about by the Great Depression. The federal government tried to help by creating programs such as the Civilian Conservation Corps (CCC) and the Works Progress Administration (WPA). These programs provided jobs for out-of-work men and women. Members of the CCC worked in national parks and fought forest fires. The WPA built roads, bridges, schools, and public libraries.

The Great Depression affected countries all over the world. Many people lost their jobs and homes. There was no work, no money, and no hope. In Germany, the people chose a man named Adolf Hitler as their leader. He promised to make Germany powerful again. In 1939, Germany's army invaded Poland. Immediately, France and England declared war against Germany for taking over Poland. Once again, European countries took sides, and the world was at war.

When World War II (1939–1945) began, the United States again chose to stay out of the war. However, businesses could sell products to England and France. Shipbuilding, lumbering, textile manufacturing, and farm products became valuable. As factories opened, Mississippians

World War II pilots trained at the Keesler Air Force Base in Biloxi.

went back to work and earned money making cloth, processing food, and milling lumber.

On December 7, 1941, the Japanese attacked the United States Naval Base at Pearl Harbor, Hawaii. The next day, the United States joined England, Russia, and France against Germany, Italy, and Japan. New army and air force bases opened in Mississippi for training military personnel. During this period, Pascagoula, a port on the Gulf of Mexico, grew into a major shipbuilding center. Food-processing plants were built to can fish, seafood, and vegetables. Lumber mills reopened, putting even more people back to work.

MISSISSIPPI CHANGES

Many African-Americans took part in World War II. Some were in the military, while others worked in factories in major cities in both the North and South. Returning to Mississippi after the war, African-Americans wanted to end segregation—the laws that separated African-Americans from whites. They challenged Jim Crow laws that had existed for more than fifty years by protesting, marching, and refusing to obey segregation laws. Civil rights battles were fought relating to education, voting, and the use of public places. Civil rights are those freedoms that allow citizens to vote, to use public facilities, and to be treated fairly by the law.

In 1954, the United States Supreme Court made an important decision about segregation. In *Brown v. Board of Education*, the court declared that "separate but equal" schooling was not equal at all. Although this ruling was about a lawsuit brought in

The Rex Theatre in Leland was one of many segregated places in Mississippi during the late 1930s.

Kansas, it affected all states with segregated schools. Mississippi schools were ordered to desegregate, allowing children of all races and cultures to attend school together. This did not happen without protests from angry whites and the state government.

It took almost ten years before Mississippi took steps to mix races in public schools. In the early 1960s, African-American James Meredith tried to enroll in the all-white University of Mississippi. Although a federal court ordered the Mississippi government to let Meredith attend the university, the governor refused. President Kennedy sent federal guards with Meredith to force the University of Mississippi to register him as a student. Two years later, in 1964, Mississippi elementary and high schools started the slow process of desegregation.

James Meredith was escorted by United States Deputy Marshals as he attended his first class at the University of Mississippi.

During the 1960s, several Mississippi African-Americans became well-known leaders in the Civil Rights movement. Medgar and Charles Evers encouraged African-Americans to stop buying goods and services from businesses that treated African-Americans badly. They also worked to register African-American voters, as did Fannie Lou Hamer, who had once been a sharecropper.

In June 1963, Medgar Evers was shot and killed in front of his home in Jackson. The shotgun used by Byron de la Beckwith was found shortly after the murder, with de la Beckwith's fresh fingerprints on the weapon. De la Beckwith opposed equal rights for African-Americans and killed Evers to stop the Civil Rights movement in Mississippi.

At the time, Evers was an official with the National Association for the Advancement of Colored People (NAACP), a group that fought for equal rights for African-Americans. Six years later, his brother Charles became the first African-American mayor in Mississippi since 1877. Charles Evers served as mayor of Fayette. Increased numbers of African-American voters have changed the face of politics in Mississippi. Today, about 1 in 5 members of the state legislature is African-American.

Mississippi continues to grow and change. In the past thirty years, manufacturing has become the state's largest industry. Major manufacturing products in the state include transportation equipment, lumber and wood products, furniture, food processing, and clothing. Cotton is still the largest agricultural crop, and Mississippi is fourth nationally in cotton production. Rice, peanuts, pecans, sugarcane, soybeans, and hay have also become moneymakers for Mississippi's farmers. A new type of farm—a catfish farm—has given Mississippi another way to make money.

Mississippi has been a pioneer in farm-raised catfish production since 1968.

Although farming is important, the state is slowly changing from a rural to an urban way of life. By 2000, nearly half of all Mississippians lived in cities. Jackson, Biloxi, and Hattiesburg have shown the most growth, with all three cities developing a large metropolitan population.

African-Americans have continued to fight for equal rights. Desegregation in schools and public facilities has been slow to happen. In 1992, the United States Supreme Court declared that Mississippi needed to improve the racial mix of its state university system. Although African-Americans made up nearly 37 in every 100 people in Mississippi, the number of African-American students was fewer than 10 in 100. The state has tried to encourage African-American students to attend state universities by providing scholarships or jobs to worthy students.

In addition, Mississippi lawmakers voted to spend $75 million between 2001 and 2006 for upgrading three historically African-American colleges. The state had not previously spent money to repair buildings, improve libraries, or provide new technology for these schools. Lawmakers hope that improving the college facilities will encourage interest in attending these schools.

Many Mississippians still cling to their southern heritage. In 2001, Mississippi voters went to the polls to decide whether to change the state flag. The flag features a replica of the Confederate flag in the upper-left corner. Some Mississippians believe that the flag serves as a reminder of the days of slavery, and that the Confederate flag portion should be replaced by a circle of twenty white stars against a dark blue background. Others, however, feel that the flag does not represent slavery at all, but rather Southern heritage and the men who fought in the Civil War. They do not want the flag to be changed. Ultimately, more Mississippians voted in favor of keeping the old flag.

Mississippians struggle to let go of the past. The days of King Cotton and slavery will never come again. Instead, the state finds opportunity in new industries, varied farm products, and equality for all its citizens.

CHAPTER FOUR

GOVERNING MISSISSIPPI

Mississippi's constitution sets down the basic rules and laws that run the government. The constitution lists the rights of the people living in the state. It also lists the responsibilities and powers of the state government.

The first Mississippi constitution was adopted in 1817, when Mississippi became a state. Two new constitutions were adopted in 1832 and 1869. The current constitution was adopted in 1890, although many amendments, or changes, have been made since then. For example, one amendment says that governors can be elected to two terms of office in a row, which was prohibited before 1994.

Amendments are suggested by the legislature (the state's lawmaking body) or at a special meeting, called a constitutional convention. An amendment must be passed by 2 in every 3 members of the legislature.

Completed in 1903, the present state capitol is the third to be built in Jackson.

If it passes the legislature, the amendment is voted on by the people. A simple majority (51 in 100 people) must vote for the change.

The Mississippi government has three branches or parts: the legislative branch, the executive branch, and the judicial branch. The legislative branch makes new laws. The executive branch enforces the laws. The judicial branch interprets the laws and determines whether someone has broken a law. Together these branches are responsible for running the state. They balance the government so that no one branch has too much power.

Legislative sessions take place in the capitol building. The senate chamber is shown below.

LEGISLATIVE BRANCH

The legislative branch is also called the legislature. Two groups make up Mississippi's legislature: the senate and the house of representatives. The senate has 52 members and the house of representatives has 122 members. All members of the legislature serve four-year terms.

Mississippi's lawmakers meet in the capitol building in Jackson. They make laws covering a variety of topics, including taxes, education, real estate, ecology, and crimes. The legislative session is limited to 125 days in a new governor's first year in office and in even-numbered years. During odd-numbered years, the session is limited to 90 days.

MISSISSIPPI GOVERNORS

Name	Term	Name	Term
David Holmes	1817–1820	Robert Lowry, Jr.	1882–1890
George Poindexter	1820–1822	John M. Stone	1890–1896
Walter Leake	1822–1825	Alselm J. McLaurin	1896–1900
Gerard C. Brandon	1825–1826	Andrew H. Longino	1900–1904
David Holmes	1826	James K. Vardaman	1904–1908
Gerard C. Brandon	1826–1832	Edmund F. Noel	1908–1912
Abram M. Scott	1832–1833	Earl L. Brewer	1912–1916
Charles Lynch	1833	Theodore G. Bilbo	1916–1920
Hiram G. Runnels	1833–1835	Lee M. Russell	1920–1924
John A. Quitman	1835–1836	Henry L. Whitfield	1924–1927
Charles Lynch	1836–1838	Dennis Murphree	1927–1928
Alexander G. McNutt	1838–1842	Theodore G. Bilbo	1928–1932
Tilghman M. Tucker	1842–1844	Martin S. Conner	1932–1936
Albert G. Brown	1844–1848	Hugh L. White	1936–1940
Joseph M. Matthews	1848–1850	Paul B. Johnson, Sr.	1940–1943
John A. Quitman	1850–1851	Dennis Murphree	1943–1944
John I. Guion	1851	Thomas L. Bailey	1944–1946
James Whitfield	1851–1852	Fielding L. Wright	1946–1952
Henry S. Foote	1852–1854	Hugh L. White	1952–1956
John J. Pettus	1854	James P. Coleman	1956–1960
John J. McRae	1854–1857	Ross R. Barnett	1960–1964
William McWillie	1857–1859	Paul B. Johnson, Jr.	1964–1968
John J. Pettus	1859–1863	John Bell Williams	1968–1972
Charles Clark	1863–1865	William L. Waller, Sr.	1972–1976
William L. Sharkey	1865	Cliff Finch	1976–1980
Benjamin G. Humphreys	1865–1868	William F. Winter	1980–1984
Adelbert Ames	1868–1870	Bill Allain	1984–1988
James L. Alcorn	1870–1871	Ray Mabus	1988–1992
Ridgley C. Powers	1871–1874	Kirk Fordice	1992–2000
Adelbert Ames	1874–1876	David R. Musgrove	2000–
John M. Stone	1876–1882		

The governor heads the executive branch. The lieutenant governor, attorney general, treasurer, auditor, and secretary of state help the governor run the state. Voters elect these government officers every four years.

One of the governor's responsibilities is to form a budget. A budget is a plan for spending state money. State funds come from taxes paid by Mississippians; the money is spent on roads, schools, state police, and many other state departments. The governor must also approve or reject bills (proposed new laws) that have been passed by the legislature.

The governor appoints people to be in charge of state commissions, such as education, agriculture and commerce, public safety, and

Since 1862, all of Mississippi's governors have lived in this mansion.

transportation. There is also a commissioner of insurance, which is an uncommon state office. The commissioner of insurance runs the Mississippi Department of Insurance, which monitors life, health, automobile, home, and business insurance in the state. Health insurance, for example, covers the cost of doctor's visits, eye exams, dental visits, and hospital care. This department oversees the companies that provide insurance policies to Mississippi citizens.

JUDICIAL BRANCH

The judicial branch in Mississippi is made up of the court system. There are several levels of courts. Each level has a responsibility to ensure fair legal treatment for Mississippi's people.

Most trials are held in chancery courts or circuit courts. These trials can be criminal or civil suits. Criminal cases involve crimes such as murder, arson, or robbery. Civil cases are those in which two or more parties have a dispute based on the law, or when one person files a lawsuit against another. For example, a person hurt in a car accident might bring a lawsuit against the driver of the car that struck him or her.

The middle-level court is the court of appeals. This court has ten judges, and each serves an eight-year term. These judges hear appeals. An appeal is the review of a decision that was made in a lower court. A person who stood trial in a circuit court may have reason to file an appeal for a new trial with the court of appeals. For example, a person could file an appeal if someone gave evidence against him or her that was proven false.

MISSISSIPPI STATE GOVERNMENT

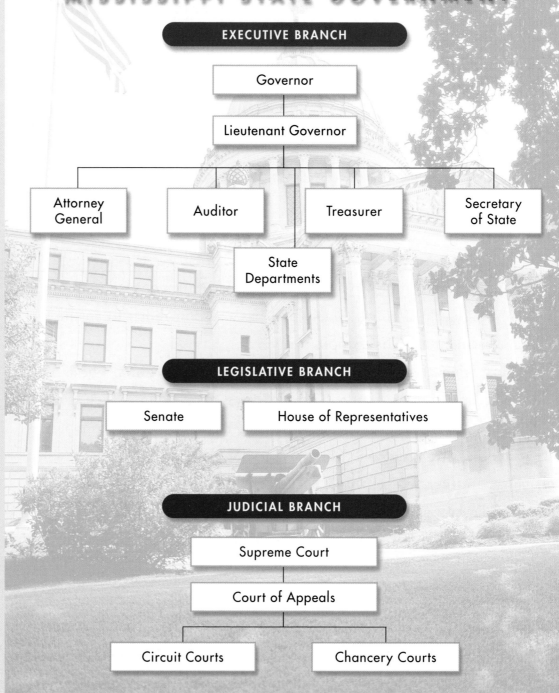

EXECUTIVE BRANCH

Governor

Lieutenant Governor

Attorney General

Auditor

Treasurer

Secretary of State

State Departments

LEGISLATIVE BRANCH

Senate

House of Representatives

JUDICIAL BRANCH

Supreme Court

Court of Appeals

Circuit Courts

Chancery Courts

Suppose a witness claimed to see a man commit a crime. If, after the trial, it is discovered that this person was not at the crime scene and could not have seen the crime committed, then an appeal could be filed.

The supreme court is the most important court in the judicial branch. The court's justices (judges) are elected from state districts. Voters elect the justices to eight-year terms. The justice who has been on the supreme court for the longest period of time serves as chief justice. It is the supreme court's job to decide if the state's laws follow the constitution and to ensure that citizens' rights are being protected.

ELECTIONS

People who want to run for state office must meet requirements set by the state. For example, a person running for governor must be at least thirty years old. He or she must have been a United States citizen for at least twenty years and have lived in Mississippi for at least five years. The requirements for each office are listed in the Mississippi constitution.

Candidates (people who run for office) need to collect signatures of voters who want them to run for office. A candidate for governor must collect one thousand signatures. Candidates for state senator or representative need to collect fifty signatures. Candidates who belong to specific political parties pay a fee to run for office.

On election day, voters cast their ballots, or votes, choosing candidates for state offices, such as governor, lieutenant governor, state senator or representative, or attorney general. Voters must be eighteen years old and a resident of the state, county, and voting district for at least 30 days. Voters must register with the state in order to vote. People can register to vote at a county clerk's or city clerk's office, or when getting a driver license.

TAKE A TOUR OF JACKSON, THE STATE CAPITAL

Jackson is a bustling industrial town that serves as the capital of Mississippi and the county government center for Hinds County. Jackson is also the largest city in the state, with a population of about 184,256 people. The city lies on the banks of the Pearl River, and is located almost in the center of the state.

Many large corporations are headquartered in Jackson.

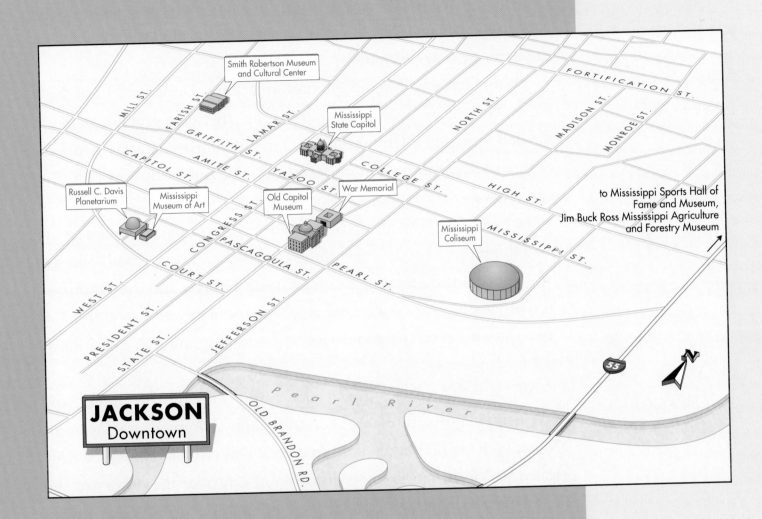

The city was originally founded in 1792 as a trading post, called LeFleur's Bluff. In 1822, Mississippi named the city as capital and changed its name to Jackson, after General Andrew Jackson, the hero of the Battle of New Orleans.

History has not always been kind to Jackson. During the Civil War, Union General W. T. Sherman burned the city to the ground, giving it the odd nickname, "Chimneyville." Today, Confederate army trenches, or ditches, can still be seen in Battlefield Park, one of the city's historic attractions.

Jackson owes most of its growth to being both a river port and a railroad shipping center. It is also along the Natchez Trace, a road followed by colonial settlers heading westward from Georgia and the Carolinas. Today, Jackson is the industrial center of the state and home to more than three hundred companies. It is also a leading cultural, educational, and medical center.

When visiting Jackson, start your tour with the Jim Buck Ross Mississippi Agriculture and Forestry/National Agricultural Aviation Museum. It is a mouthful—and an eyeful. This unusual museum is dedicated to Mississippi farming history. You can trace the history of the state's farmers and lumberjacks, see mechanical cotton-picking inventions from the 1800s, and learn about the development of tractors. You can also learn about cropdusters and how they zoomed over fields, dropping pesticides to kill insects and fertilizers to help crops grow. There are farm buildings with live animals and a realistic 1920s Mississippi town, complete with a general store, sawmill, and school.

The capitol building, built between 1901 and 1903, houses the legislature and executive offices. The capitol building is a beautiful blend of marble, stone, and stained glass. Inside, tour the Hall of Governors, where visitors can see portraits of Mississippi's past leaders. This was the first building in Mississippi to have full electrical service.

Next stop is the nearby War Memorial and the State Historical Museum, now the Old Capitol Museum. The War Memorial honors veterans from many wars. The memorial features a model of the Tomb of the Unknown Soldier and has a museum devoted to Mississippi's past military efforts. The Old Capitol building, built in the 1830s, was

CHAPTER FIVE

THE PEOPLE AND PLACES OF MISSISSIPPI

Matthew Smith and Jim Mark provide musical entertainment at the Farmers Market in Oxford.

About 2,844,658 people live in Mississippi. The overall population of Mississippi ranks thirty-first among all states. Roughly 62 in every 100 Mississippians are of European descent. Of these, most trace their relatives back to Ireland, England, and Germany.

Another 36 in 100 people are African-American. Fewer than 2 in 100 are Asian American, Native American, or Hispanic. In the past ten years, the Hispanic population has more than doubled, from 15,931 in 1990 to 39,569 in 2000.

The Native Americans in Mississippi are largely Choctaw. Many Choctaw live on the Mississippi Choctaw Indian Reservation, located in Neshoba County near the Alabama border. The United States government recognized this group in 1918 and granted them land. Continued growth of minority groups will add diversity to the Mississippi population.

Beautiful neighborhoods with tree-lined streets grace Mississippi suburbs.

Since colonial days, most Mississippians have lived in rural environments, on farms or in small towns. In the past ten years, slightly more than half of all Mississippians have become city or suburban dwellers. This is a major change for a state that has long survived on agriculture. The most populated areas in the state include Jackson, Biloxi, Gulfport, and Hattiesburg. Even so, Mississippi has only one city—Jackson—with a population of more than 100,000.

THE ARTS IN THE SOUTH

From the early days of settlement, music filled the air of Mississippi's fields, churches, and homes. Plantation workers chanted as they worked and sang spirituals drawn from their African heritage. The English and

FIND OUT MORE

A metropolitan area is made up of a city and its suburbs (nearby towns and villages). Jackson has a population of 184,256 people. The metropolitan area has a population of about 440,801. How many people live in the suburbs of Jackson?

Scots played reels and country songs brought from their homeland. The music of Mississippi contributed to the formation of jazz, blues, and rock and roll.

Today, the state proudly claims a tradition of fine musicians and singers. Blues guitarists Bo Diddley and B. B. King, opera singer Leontyne Price, and jazz singer Muddy Waters are all from Mississippi. Tupelo's Elvis Presley based his musical style on a mixture of rock and roll and gospel tradition. Today, country and western stars LeAnn Rimes, Jimmy Buffet, and Faith Hill add greater dimensions to Mississippi's musical heritage.

The dramatic arts have also spotlighted Mississippi's many talented African-Americans. Actress and television host Oprah Winfrey of

WHO'S WHO IN MISSISSIPPI?

B. B. King (1925–) is an internationally known blues guitarist and singer. Although he made his living as a musician from an early age, he did not become well known until the mid-1960s, when the Beatles first heard King play. He is considered by some to be the world's greatest blues guitarist. King was born in Indianola.

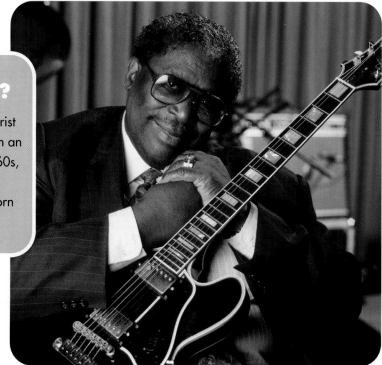

Kosciusko can be seen daily on her television talk show, *Oprah*. Likewise, James Earl Jones of Arkabutla has been seen in Shakespearean plays, on Broadway, and in movies and television. Another leading African-American actor who grew up in Mississippi, Morgan Freeman, has been praised for his acting in such movies as *Glory* and *Driving Miss Daisy*. Other famous performers from Mississippi include Sela Ward, Gerald McRaney, and Jim Henson, creator of the Muppets.

THE WRITTEN WORD

The state has also enjoyed its share of acclaimed writers, historians, and playwrights. Perhaps the most honored was William Faulkner, who wrote novels and stories set in rural Mississippi.

Short stories by writer Eudora Welty give a gentle view of daily life in Mississippi. Welty won the 1973 Pulitzer Prize in fiction for *The Optimist's Daughter*. The African-American view of Mississippi life is portrayed by novelist Richard Wright in his autobiography, *Black Boy*. Adding to the rich tradition of Deep South writings are playwrights Beth Henley and Tennessee Williams, writer Willie Morris, and best-selling novelist John Grisham.

WHO'S WHO IN MISSISSIPPI?

William Faulkner (1897–1962) won the Nobel Prize for literature in 1949. His novels, *A Fable* and *The Reivers*, also won Pulitzer Prizes. Among Faulkner's best-known works are *Light in August, The Sound and the Fury,* and *Absalom, Absalom!* Faulkner was born in New Albany.

Since the late 1930s, Mississippi's government has worked to help the state's economy by bringing in new industries and promoting variety in agriculture. Strangely, the state that grew wealthy because of cotton also grew poor because of the same crop. The people relied too heavily on having a good crop of quality, high-priced cotton. When the boll weevil destroyed cotton crops, farmers and fieldworkers had no other source of income. Today, service industries, manufacturing, retail, and agriculture all play a role in the state's economy.

Farming continues to provide jobs and money to the state. As with most other states, Mississippi's farms are becoming fewer in number but larger in size. About 7 in 10 farms are dedicated to poultry, dairy products, or livestock.

A farmer harvests sweet potatoes in a field near Houston.

The greatest moneymakers are cotton, broiler chickens, soybeans, and beef cattle. Pecans and peanuts, sweet potatoes, rice, and watermelons add variety to the state's agricultural product base. Along the Mississippi River, a new industry has blossomed—aquaculture, or the farming of fish and seafood. Catfish, trout, and other seafood "farms" provide employment for a very different kind of farmer—a fish farmer. About 10 in every 100 workers are farmers.

In 1965, factory and industry workers outnumbered farmers for the first time in the state's history. Today, manufacturing employs 25 in 100 workers. Transportation equipment is the largest manufacturing industry, followed by electrical equipment, food processing, clothing, and chemicals. The southern part of the state has major shipbuilding and commercial fishing industries, as well as canneries for shrimp, fish, and oysters. Canneries process fish and seafood, putting the finished products in cans or in frozen packaging. The Gulf Coast is also home to the John C. Stennis Space Center, one of ten NASA testing centers in the United States.

Located in Hancock County, the John C. Stennis Space Center tests engines that power space shuttles.

59

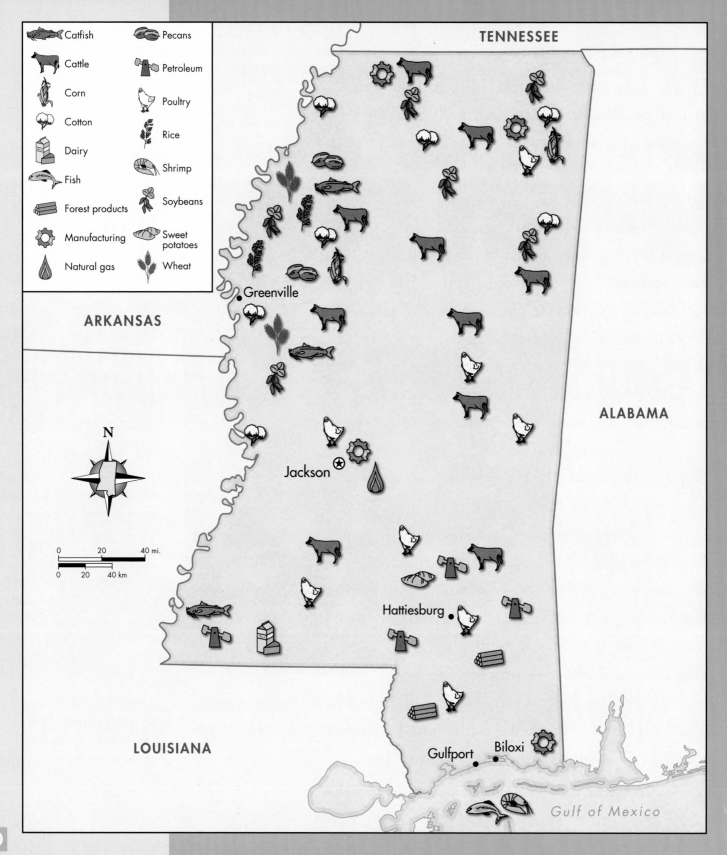

Catfish
Cattle
Corn
Cotton
Dairy
Fish
Forest products
Manufacturing
Natural gas
Pecans
Petroleum
Poultry
Rice
Shrimp
Soybeans
Sweet potatoes
Wheat

TENNESSEE

ARKANSAS

ALABAMA

Greenville

N

0   20   40 mi.
0   20   40 km

Jackson

Hattiesburg

LOUISIANA

Gulfport   Biloxi

Gulf of Mexico

60

In central Mississippi, Jackson and Meridian are home to electrical, computer, and service industries. A Nissan car factory is located near Jackson. In the northeastern part of the state, where cotton is grown, textile plants provide income for many workers.

Mississippi makes good use of its natural resources. In the south-western part of the state, natural gas and oil wells are found. Gypsum and salt are mined in southern Mississippi, while the state's forests provide lumber for wood pulp, paper, and furniture.

Tourism is a growth industry in Mississippi. The state attracts many vacationers to its beaches, riverboats, and parks. In 1990, voters approved a law allowing gambling (playing cards, dice, or other games for money) in their state. Gambling has become a major moneymaker for Mississippi. Today, gaming casinos in Tunica, Vicksburg, Natchez, Philadelphia, Biloxi, Gulfport, and Bay St. Louis draw thousands of tourists and plenty of money. State income from the casinos goes toward education, recreation, and other state programs.

Riverboat casinos are a popular form of entertainment along the Gulf Coast.

Black-eyed peas are a southern tradition. Serve them with baked ham, sweet potatoes, and corn bread. Use the corn bread to sop up the pea juice, called "liquor" in Mississippi. Ask an adult for help with the recipe below.

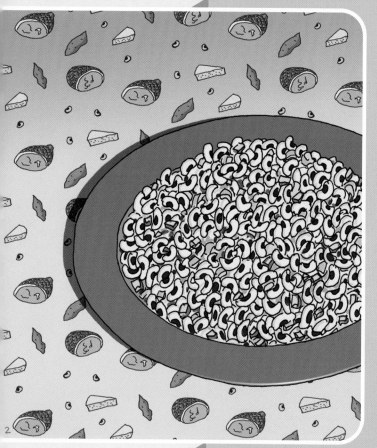

BLACK-EYED PEAS

1 pound dried black-eyed peas
2 quarts water
1 medium onion, chopped
1/4 cup green pepper, chopped
1 rib celery, chopped
1/2 cup ham or bacon, chopped
salt and pepper, to taste

1. Wash the dried peas under cold, running water. Place in a bowl and cover with water. Let sit overnight.
2. Drain off the soaking water. Place peas in a large pot with 2 quarts of water.
3. Add onion, pepper, celery, and ham or bacon.
4. Cover and bring to a boil. Reduce heat and let peas simmer on low heat for 2 hours or until peas are soft. You may need to add more water as the peas cook. Add hot water, one cup at a time, being careful to add just enough water to cover the peas.
5. Add salt and pepper to taste. Begin by adding 1 teaspoon salt and 1/2 teaspoon pepper. Stir, then taste with a clean spoon. Season more if needed. Makes 4–6 servings.

Western Mississippi

Let's begin our tour at the source of the state's name: the Mississippi River, the father of waters. Natchez is your starting point, and there's plenty to see and do. Each year Natchez holds pilgrimages where people can tour the many beautiful antebellum homes there. These events recall the history of the South and the African-American musical tradition. Visitors can enjoy singing, dancing, southern-style food, and craft fairs.

Be sure to visit the Grand Village of the Natchez Indians. This site features the ceremonial mound and main village of the Natchez people. The museum exhibits Native American artifacts from the tribe, and depicts the daily lives of the Natchez people in the 1700s.

Visitors can see a reconstructed thatched house and corn granary at the Grand Village of the Natchez.

The Illinois State Memorial, shown right, is one of approximately 1,400 monuments at Vicksburg National Military Park.

All aboard! Catch a paddlewheeler or old-fashioned riverboat and experience Mississippi River life from Natchez to the Tennessee border. Along the way, stop at Vicksburg, the site of one of the worst sieges of the Civil War. The Vicksburg National Military Park and Cemetery has monuments to Union and Confederate armies on the memorial battle-field. Vicksburg also has many elegant homes and Civil War museums, such as the Old Court House Museum, open to tourists. These sites will give you a true feeling for the Old South.

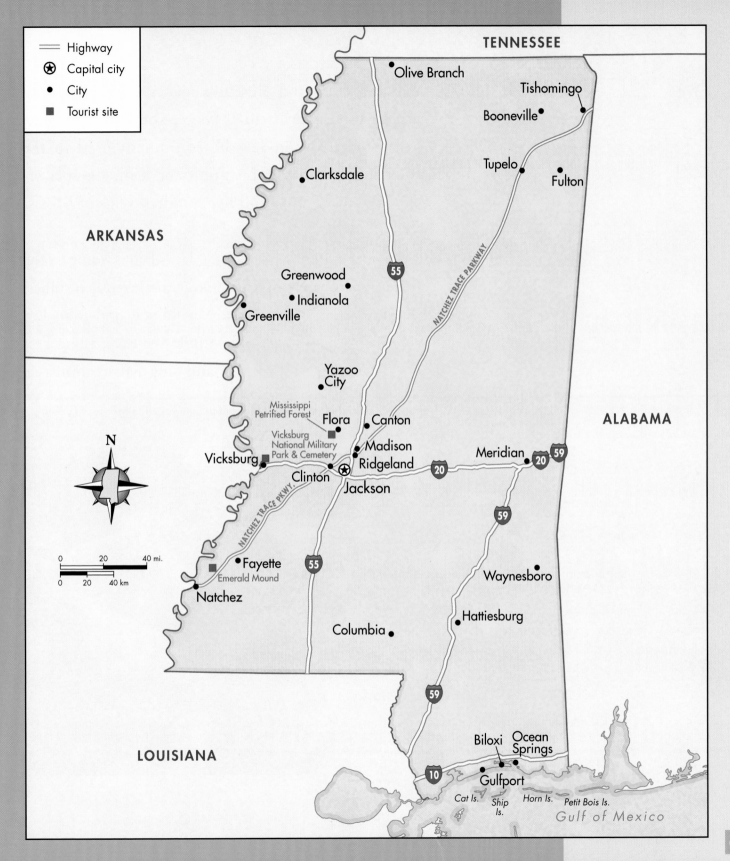

TENNESSEE

ARKANSAS

ALABAMA

LOUISIANA

Olive Branch

Tishomingo

Booneville

Clarksdale

Tupelo

Fulton

Greenwood

Indianola

Greenville

NATCHEZ TRACE PARKWAY

Yazoo City

55

Mississippi Petrified Forest

Flora

Canton

Vicksburg National Military Park & Cemetery

Madison

Ridgeland

Meridian

20   59

Vicksburg

Clinton

Jackson

20

NATCHEZ TRACE PKWY.

59

N

Fayette

55

Waynesboro

Emerald Mound

Natchez

Hattiesburg

0   20   40 mi.

0   20   40 km

Columbia

59

Biloxi   Ocean Springs

10

Gulfport

Cat Is.

Ship Is.

Horn Is.

Petit Bois Is.

Gulf of Mexico

If touring stately mansions and museums makes you thirsty, stop by the Biedenharn Coca-Cola Museum. There, you can learn how Coca-Cola® was first bottled and see the equipment used in the process. At the waterfront, catch a jet-boat tour and learn about river-bank wildlife, Civil War adventures, and five hundred years of Mississippi River history.

Music fans hit the big time in Mississippi. Clarksdale is home to the Delta Blues Museum, where you can learn about the legends of blues: W. C. Handy, Muddy Waters, B. B. King, Ma Rainey, and John Lee Hooker. If you're there in August, catch the Sunflower River Blues Festival where blues musicians gather to play and sing Mississippi-style blues and jazz.

WHO'S WHO IN MISSISSIPPI?

Muddy Waters (1915–1983), born McKinley Morganfield, was a blues guitar player, singer, and songwriter. His nickname comes from the "muddy Mississippi waters." His link to his Mississippi heritage is heard in his albums, *The Real Folk Blues* and *They Call Me Muddy Waters.* Waters was born in Rolling Fork.

Eastern Mississippi

After Clarksdale, head east to Tupelo, home of "the King," Elvis Presley. Presley's childhood home is now part of the Elvis Presley Center and Museum. In Tupelo, you can pick up the Natchez Trace, nicknamed the Devil's Backbone because it was dangerous for travelers in the 1700s and 1800s. This highway ran between Natchez and Nashville, Tennessee, and was the main route for early settlers heading west to the Mississippi. You won't find outlaws or poisonous snakes along the Natchez Trace today, but you will get a sense of the Mississippi countryside.

Along the way, stop at Emerald Mound, one of the nation's largest earthworks mounds. You'll also want to visit the Chickasaw village site near Tupelo. There you can learn about native foods and medicines.

Southern Mississippi

The Gulf Coast region also holds many attractions. In Biloxi, you can tour Jefferson Davis' home, Beauvoir, in the morning, then go deep-sea fishing in the afternoon. Biloxi is Old South, with three centuries of history visible in its shaded avenues, parks, and buildings. Shrimp fans—

WHO'S WHO IN MISSISSIPPI?

Elvis Presley (1935–1977) was a legendary rock and roll and gospel singer as well as a movie actor. Called "the King," Presley had many number-one songs and made thirty movies. His songs included "Love Me Tender," "Jailhouse Rock," and "Blue Suede Shoes." Presley was born in Tupelo.

this place is for you. You can take a Biloxi shrimping trip aboard the *Sailfish,* and get firsthand experience in the art of shrimp fishing. The port also offers gulf cruises aboard large sailboats called schooners. At the Maritime and Seafood Industry Museum, you can learn about the history and the challenge of commercial fishing.

Take a boat trip to beautiful Ship Island. This is the home of historic Fort Massachusetts. There are long secluded stretches of beach and sparkling clean, gulf water for swimming. Dolphin watching is quite common, as these marine mammals love to swim alongside tourist boats.

Tourists enjoy sunbathing on Ship Island.

Finally, a unique experience for the whole family is a trip to the Mississippi Petrified Forest near Flora. There, you can take a self-guided tour of petrified trees that are more than 36 million years old. Petrified trees were regular trees that have turned into rock over time. The earth science museum offers displays of rocks, minerals, and fossils specific to Mississippi.

Summers are hot in Mississippi, so bring your sunscreen and a wide-brimmed hat. Sit beneath a sprawling live oak and watch Spanish moss sway in the gentle Gulf breezes. This is Mississippi at its best. Come on down and sit a spell. Y'all are welcome!

MISSISSIPPI ALMANAC

Statehood date and number: December 10, 1817; twentieth state

State seal: A gold eagle against a white background. The eagle bears olive branches as a sign of peace. On the eagle's breast is a red, white, and blue shield that represents the United States flag. Adopted in 1817.

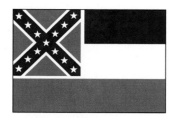

State flag: The upper-left corner features the Confederate battle flag. The rest is taken from the Stars and Bars, the first flag of the Confederate States of America. The "bars" are three wide horizontal stripes—one blue, one white, and one red. Adopted in 1894.

Geographic center: Leake, 9 miles (14 km) WNW of Carthage

Total area/rank: 48,434 square miles (125,444 sq km)/32nd

Coastline/rank: 44 miles (71 km)/19th

Borders: Tennessee, Alabama, Arkansas, Louisiana, Gulf of Mexico

Latitude and longitude: Mississippi is located approximately between 30° 13' and 35° 00' N and 88° 07' and 91° 41' W.

Highest/lowest elevation: Woodall Mountain, 806 feet (246 m)/Gulf of Mexico, sea level

Hottest/coldest temperature: 115° F (46° C) at Holly Springs on July 29, 1930/−19° F (−28° C) at Corinth on January 30, 1966

Land area/rank: 46,914 square miles (121,507 sq km)/31st

Inland water area: 1,520 square miles (3,937 sq km)

Population/rank (2000 census): 2,844,658/31st

Population of major cities:

   Jackson: 184,256

   Gulfport: 71,127

   Biloxi: 50,644

   Hattiesburg: 44,779

   Greenville: 41,663

Origin of state name: Named for the Mississippi River

State capital: Jackson

Counties: 82

State government: 52 senators, 122 representatives

Rivers/lakes: Mississippi, Yazoo, Pascagoula, Pearl, Tallahatchie, Big Sunflower, Big Black, and Tombigbee/Ross Barnett Reservoir, Beulah, Moon, Lee, and Washington

Farm products: Cotton, milk, soybeans, corn, hay, rice, wheat, timber, sweet potatoes, pecans, watermelons, peanuts

Livestock: Milk cows, beef cattle, hogs

Manufacturing products: Transportation equipment, food products, paper products, furniture, clothing, wood products, electrical equipment, chemicals

Mining products: Natural gas, oil, gypsum, salt, clay, sand, sandstone, iron ore, lignite, limestone

Fishing products: Shrimp, buffalofish, carp, catfish

Beverage: Milk

Bird: Mockingbird

Butterfly: Spicebush swallowtail

Fish: Largemouth bass

Flower: Magnolia

Fossil: Zygorhiza kochii, a prehistoric whale

Insect: Honey bee

Land mammal: White-tailed deer

Motto: "By Valor and Arms"

Nickname: Magnolia State

Shell: Oyster

Song: "Go, Mississippi"; words and music by Houston Davis

Stone: Petrified wood

Tree: Magnolia

Water mammal: Bottle-nosed dolphin

Wildlife: White-tailed deer, squirrels, muskrats, beavers, raccoons, opossums, foxes, wild turkeys, quail, wild doves, mockingbirds, cranes, egrets, brown pelicans

TIMELINE

MISSISSIPPI STATE HISTORY

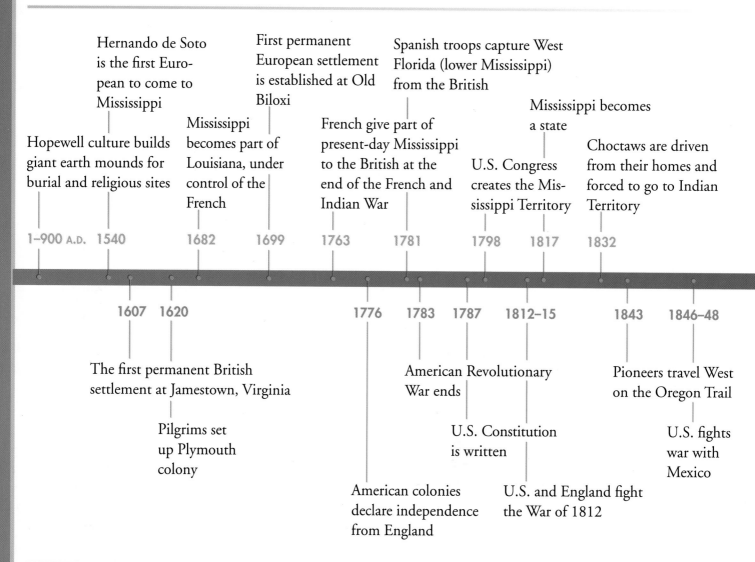

Hernando de Soto is the first European to come to Mississippi

First permanent European settlement is established at Old Biloxi

Spanish troops capture West Florida (lower Mississippi) from the British

Mississippi becomes a state

Hopewell culture builds giant earth mounds for burial and religious sites

Mississippi becomes part of Louisiana, under control of the French

French give part of present-day Mississippi to the British at the end of the French and Indian War

U.S. Congress creates the Mississippi Territory

Choctaws are driven from their homes and forced to go to Indian Territory

| 1–900 A.D. | 1540 | 1682 | 1699 | 1763 | 1781 | 1798 | 1817 | 1832 |

| 1607 | 1620 | 1776 | 1783 | 1787 | 1812–15 | 1843 | 1846–48 |

The first permanent British settlement at Jamestown, Virginia

American Revolutionary War ends

Pioneers travel West on the Oregon Trail

Pilgrims set up Plymouth colony

U.S. Constitution is written

U.S. fights war with Mexico

American colonies declare independence from England

U.S. and England fight the War of 1812

UNITED STATES HISTORY

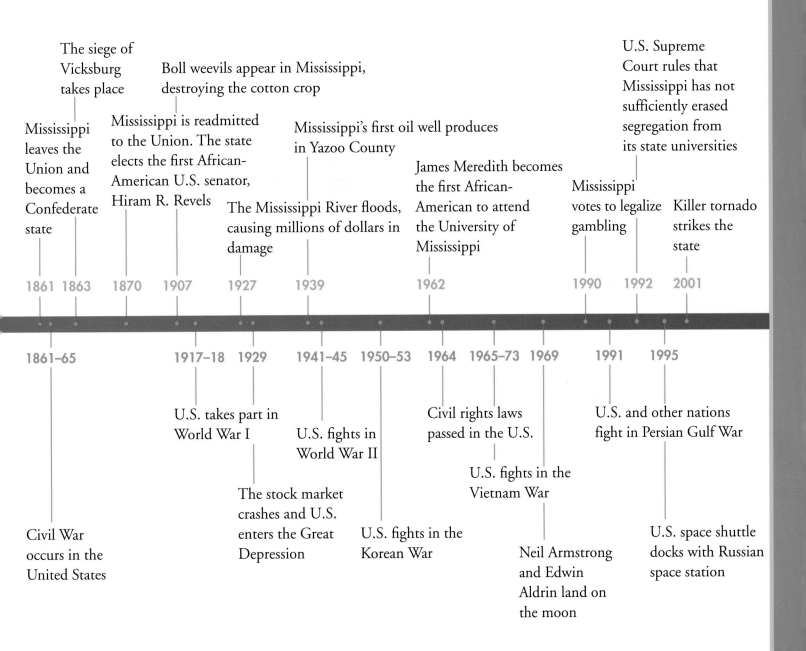

The siege of
Vicksburg
takes place

Boll weevils appear in Mississippi,
destroying the cotton crop

U.S. Supreme
Court rules that
Mississippi has not
sufficiently erased
segregation from
its state universities

Mississippi
leaves the
Union and
becomes a
Confederate
state

Mississippi is readmitted
to the Union. The state
elects the first African-
American U.S. senator,
Hiram R. Revels

Mississippi's first oil well produces
in Yazoo County

James Meredith becomes
the first African-
American to attend
the University of
Mississippi

Mississippi
votes to legalize
gambling

Killer tornado
strikes the
state

The Mississippi River floods,
causing millions of dollars in
damage

1861 1863   1870   1907   1927   1939   1962   1990   1992   2001

1861–65   1917–18 1929   1941–45 1950–53 1964   1965–73 1969   1991   1995

U.S. takes part in
World War I

U.S. fights in
World War II

Civil rights laws
passed in the U.S.

U.S. and other nations
fight in Persian Gulf War

U.S. fights in the
Vietnam War

The stock market
crashes and U.S.
enters the Great
Depression

U.S. fights in the
Korean War

Civil War
occurs in the
United States

Neil Armstrong
and Edwin
Aldrin land on
the moon

U.S. space shuttle
docks with Russian
space station

GALLERY OF FAMOUS MISSISSIPPIANS

Shelby Foote
(1916–)
Novelist, historian, and play-wright. Best known for his narrative entitled *The Civil War.* Born in Greenville.

Beth Henley
(1952–)
Pulitzer prize-winning playwright for *Crimes of the Heart.* Born in Jackson.

Jim Henson
(1936–1990)
Creator of the Muppets. Known for his work on *Sesame Street.* Born in Greenville.

James Earl Jones
(1931–)
Popular movie, television, and Broadway actor. Known as the voice of Darth Vader in *Star Wars.* Born in Arkabutla.

Willie Morris
(1934–1999)
Author of many books, including *My Dog Skip, Good Old Boy,* and *The Ghosts of Medgar Evers,* all of which have been made into movies. Born in Jackson.

Robert Pittman
(1953–)
Created a cable music network called MTV. Born in Jackson.

Leontyne Price
(1927–)
American opera singer known for her work in Gershwin's *Porgy and Bess,* Verdi's *Aïda,* and Puccini's *Madame Butterfly.* Born in Laurel.

Hiram R. Revels
(1822–1901)
First African-American to serve in the United States Senate (1870–1871); he represented Mississippi.

Tennessee Williams
(1911–1983)
Pulitzer prize-winning playwright for *A Streetcar Named Desire.* Born in Columbus.

Oprah Winfrey
(1954–)
Television entertainer, actress, and publisher. Star of her own TV show. Born in Kosciusko.

Richard Wright
(1908–1960)
Author of *Native Son* and *Black Boy.* Also, a poet and essayist. Born near Natchez.

Emmett York
(1903–1971)
Developed the Choctaw High School in Pearl River. Established the United Southeastern Tribes, a Native American council. Born in Standing Pine.

GLOSSARY

alluvial: having to do with soil deposited by floods or rivers

amendment: a change in a law or document

antebellum: existing before the Civil War

appeal: a request to have a higher court review a trial and its legality

aquaculture: farming fish or seafood

capital: the city that is the center of a state or country government

capitol: the building in which a government meets

climate: an area's weather conditions over a long period of time

constitution: basic rules and laws that run a government

delta: a triangle of land formed when a river spreads out and divides as it empties into a large body of water

economy: a system of producing and distributing money

hummock: a small island of land in wetlands or swamp

levee: a dike or earthworks to hold back river water

livestock: beef cattle, hogs, poultry, or dairy cows; live animals on a farm

manufacturing: making products in mass quantities, such as cars or lamps

plantation: a large farm dedicated to one main crop, such as cotton

population: the number and mix of people in a region

recede: to draw back; withdraw

reservoir: a human-made lake where water is collected and stored to be used for hydroelectric power, irrigation, or other purposes

secede: to leave or withdraw from a group

transportation: a system of roads, trains, buses, and airports

unemployment: the condition of being out of work

FOR MORE INFORMATION

Web sites

The State of Mississippi
http://www.state.ms.us/
Information about the state.

Mississippi Department of Archives and History
http://www.mdah.state.ms.us/
Historic papers and magazine articles about the state.

Mississippi History Now
http://mshistory.k12.ms.us/
Information about the history of Mississippi.

Civil Rights Documentation Project
http://www-dept.usm.edu/~mcrohb/
The writings and recordings of people who fought for civil rights.

Books

Fireside, Harvey. *The Mississippi Burning Civil Rights Murder Conspiracy Trial: A Headline Court Case.* Berkeley Heights, NJ: Enslow, 2002.

Fraser, Mary Ann. *Vicksburg: The Battle that Won the Civil War.* New York, NY: Henry Holt, 1999.

George, Linda and Charles. *The Natchez Trace.* Danbury, CT: Children's Press, 2001.

Lauber, Patricia. *Flood: Wrestling with the Mississippi.* Washington, DC: National Geographic Society, 1996.

Marsh, Carole. *Mississippi Indians!: A Kid's Look at Our State's Chiefs, Tribes, Reservations, Powwows, Lore & More from the Past & the Present.* Peachtree City, GA: Gallopade Publishing, 1995.

Addresses

Mississippi Division of Tourism
P. O. Box 1705
Ocean Spring, MS 39566

Mississippi Department of Economic and Community Development
P. O. Box 849
Jackson, MS 39205

Metro Jackson Convention and Visitors Bureau
921 N. President Street
Jackson, MS 39215

Natchez Convention and Visitors Bureau
640 S. Canal Street, Box C
Natchez, MS 39120

INDEX

ABOUT THE AUTHOR

Barbara A. Somervill enjoys writing for children. She says, "The challenge is to find interesting information and present it in a way that children can understand and enjoy." Finding Mississippi information meant checking out a number of sources, such as the Internet, Chambers of Commerce and tourist bureaus, and the local library.

Barbara was raised and educated in New York State. She's also lived in Toronto, Canada; Canberra, Australia; Palo Alto, California; and Simpsonville, South Carolina. She is the mother of four boys, two dogs, and a cat, and the proud grandmother of Lilly.